OPEN STUDIO: TEN YEARS

D1435747

Dedicated to Nick Novak
1954–September 1980

OPEN STUDIO: TEN YEARS

Open Studio Toronto 1980

The Art Gallery at Harbourfront
October 3–November 2, 1980

Exhibition circulated by Art Gallery of Ontario
Extension Services, 1981-1982

ISBN 0-9690485-0-5

Design: Scott Thornley
Exhibition photographs: Michael Mitchell
Open Studio production photographs: Paul Feldman
Editor: Cathleen Hoskins
Project coordinator: Cyndra MacDowall

Art Gallery at Harbourfront director: Anita Aarons
Art Gallery at Harbourfront curator: Richard Sinclair

Coordinator of touring exhibition: Glenda Milrod,
    Exhibition Producer, Art Gallery of Ontario
    Extension Services

Typesetting: Crocker Bryant Inc.
Colour separations: Prolith
Printing: Gilchrist-Wright Ltd.

Canadian Cataloguing in Publication Data

Open Studio.
Open Studio: ten years

Exhibition circulated by Art Gallery of Ontario
Extension Services, 1981-1982.
Bibliography: p.
ISBN 0-9690485-0-5

1. Prints, Canadian–Exhibitions. 2. Prints–20th
century–Canada–Exhibitions. 3. Etching, Canadian–
Exhibitions. 4. Etching–20th century–Canada–
Exhibitions. 5. Lithography, Canadian–Exhibitions.
6. Lithography–20th century–Canada–Exhibitions.
I. Title: Open Studio: ten years.
NE541.4.063   769.971'074'011   C80-094787-8

Open Studio
520 King Street West
Toronto, Ontario M5V 1L7

The frontispiece photograph shows the first Open
Studio Graphic Sturges etching press, owned by
Barbara Hall.

William Kurelek, *Children Schoolbound in Northern B.C.*

CONTENTS

ACKNOWLEDGEMENTS

Our thanks to the following sponsors for their generous contributions to Open Studio:

The Samuel and Saidye Bronfman Family Foundation
Cadillac Fairview Corporation
The Canada Council
Corporation of Metropolitan Toronto
The Eaton Foundation
Imperial Oil
Charles H. Ivey Foundation
Labatt's Ontario Breweries Ltd.
The Laidlaw Foundation
The McLean Foundation
F.K. Morrow Foundation
The Ontario Arts Council
Stelco Inc.

We would also like to thank the many people who have contributed time, energy and assistance towards the Open Studio Tenth Anniversary Exhibition Program.

Lorna Livey, *Piano Window*

OPEN STUDIO: UNIQUE RECORDING STUDIO FOR THE VISUAL ARTS

Somewhere in this catalogue, among all the historical information, the technical procedures, the artists' biographies and the critical overview of the history of prints, a simple question has to be asked: "What is Open Studio and why does it exist?" Not why does it exist at all, but why at this moment in history and why in Toronto?

Over the past ten years a dozen or so print facilities have grown up across Canada. Also, a wide variety of artist co-ops similar in structure to the corporate umbrella of Open Studio have served a number of artistic needs. But unlike the majority of these organizations, Open Studio is a *professional production situation*. To state that Open Studio is a "print workshop" or a "printmaking facility" will be misunderstood. These labels are misunderstood because the print scene and the marketplace where these terms are used is misunderstood. Not all prints are created equal. Not all prints have the same essence of personal involvement by the artists as do the prints produced at Open Studio. This involvement or engagement of the artist is a constant force at Open Studio and, consequently, an ingredient in all prints produced at the studio. It is this involvement that will eventually be seen as an historically unique rationale for the importance of the works created during Open Studio's existence. It is this personal, artistic involvement as an ingredient of all Open Studio prints that sets these prints apart from the grey market in which they compete. This same involvement will eventually be seen as the element that makes the operation of Open Studio unique.

Open Studio is a "recording studio" that makes two-dimensional visual records called prints. There are many similarities between an audio record created in a recording studio and played and purchased in a music store and a print created in a printing facility and viewed and purchased in a gallery. For example, an audio record may differ from a live performance of music in ways similar to the different visual solutions found in printmaking in contrast to drawing or painting. Artists who have the need and ability to realize their ideas in a recording mode are called "recording artists" in the audio world, and in the visual world these recording artists are called "printmakers".

Open Studio is unique because within its corporate structure the artist has the potential to perform not only the role of artist, but also of technician, publisher and, perhaps most importantly, of producer of his or her own ideas. Open Studio's unusual development has been possible because of two influences peculiar to Canada: one on the national, historical level and one, local and contemporary.

The overall history of prints and printing is not the same in Europe, in the United States and in Canada. To oversimplify, the impetus for the production of most of the prints in Europe came from a management situation that reflected primarily the needs of the publisher. The publisher decided on the project, and printers and artists were hired or commissioned to participate as needed. In the United States the production of prints arose from a situation that reflected the management arrangements of printers. The printer-as-publisher became the norm there as master printers founded print facilities and then invited artists whose work would allow the printer to display his technical virtuosity.

In Canada, however, prints and printing have largely remained in the hands of the artists, and here printmaking is really a cottage industry. Of all the printshops existent over the past decade in Canada, only one, the print workshop at the Nova Scotia College of Art and Design, was initiated by a master printer who was not also an artist. Open Studio and all the others have followed the tradition begun in the 1950s by Richard Lacroix when he founded Guilde Graphique in Montreal: a print workshop developed by *artists* to meet the needs of the artists who use it to create and record their ideas.

In terms of structure, Open Studio has benefitted most from the fact that in Toronto at this precise time a large number of artists are developing their own corporate structures. These corporate structures are becoming personal tools that help artists create, fund, support and exhibit their ideas. In these corporate structures the artist is not a guest, nor an employee, nor a customer, nor a client, but is proprietor, producer and management.

Over the last ten years Open Studio has been able to integrate two very unusual Canadian phenomena: the rise of Canadian prints as a cottage industry and the tentative beginnings of the use of the corporate structure by the artists themselves. This combination has made Open Studio unique in this city.

Richard Sewell

Terry Legault, *Triumph (Triptych)*

It all began in August 1970, when two out-of-work, part-time printmakers plunked down the first month's rent for a dingy and potentially dangerous little storefront on Queen Street West. It hardly seemed an ideal moment to set up shop, since they had just lost their jobs as framing and gallery assistants at the Adam and Yves Gallery on Markham Street when Yves Cousineau sold out his business. (He was to prove an invaluable ally throughout the following nine years.) Despite a lack of windows and ventilation, an acid bath in the washroom and only a small Sturges etching press, Richard Sewell and Barbara Hall were determined to make the space work. They planned to teach drawing, painting, dressmaking and their own *raisons d'etre*—etching and screenprinting—to make the studio pay for itself.

Financing was a constant problem. Hall and Sewell scrounged left-over materials and equipment, pooled their unemployment insurance receipts, taught classes and did custom printing to keep the studio afloat. But from the beginning the rental of printmaking facilities was an important source of revenue, and artists and students sharing the facilities chipped in to pay the landlord. Fortunately, a few other people were also willing to donate time and energy during these early days. John Street provided advertising leaflets for the studio, and Nikolette Jakovac helped with the business end of things.

Throughout 1970 and 1971 the small studio began to attract people interested in printmaking, and in April 1971 Hall and Sewell organized a large party, designed to bring their work and shop to the attention of the arts community. Also in 1971 Don Holman, a lithographer living in Chicago, visited the storefront studio and expressed interest in the possibility of joining forces with Hall and Sewell. The next year, with the help of a Local Initiatives Project grant, Holman was invited to come to Toronto to research and set up a lithography shop.

By the time Holman's ideas for a lithography shop were being formulated, there had been a major change in the organization of the studio. In March 1972, after twenty months as a partnership, the studio was legally incorporated as a non-profit corporation with the following objectives:

1. To provide facilities and services in lithography, etching and screenprinting to Canadian artists.
2. To make these facilities available to both experienced and beginning printmakers.

3. To encourage technical and artistic excellence in printmaking by providing the best possible equipment and instruction and by maintaining professional standards of production, documentation and presentation of prints.

4. To educate the public about printmaking, through means such as exhibitions, tours, workshops and publication and sale of prints, in order to assist the growth and development of Canadian printmaking.

The name Open Studio was chosen to emphasize the founders' central concern that the entire structure of a cooperative arts facility should be open to the artists. This philosophy covers not only the use of equipment and exchange of skills but also access to and responsibility for the management and administration of the printmaking studio. A board of directors, all honorary positions, became responsible for the operation of the studio in a corporate legal sense, with Yves Cousineau serving as president from 1972 to 1979. The staff — Sewell, Hall and Holman — continued to work without salary, donating their time to keep the studio functioning.

By this time the studio had had its first formal exhibition (December 1971) of works by artists who had rented printmaking facilities during the first year. Open Studio was beginning its slow and steady flourishing. The importance of modern printmaking had begun to attract artists and collectors all over North America, and Hall, Sewell and Holman's gut feeling about the significance of the contemporary art print would soon prove boldly accurate. Before long, printmakers all over Canada would begin to take note of the high-quality works coming out of Open Studio.

But printmaking is a costly art, and money matters continued to plague the studio. With advice from Peeter Sepp, visual arts officer of the new Ontario Arts Council, Open Studio submitted its first grant request and in the spring of 1971 received its first grant of $1500 from the OAC. In the summer of 1972 the first Canada Council grant of $9000 came through, and two-thirds of that sum went to establish the lithography shop in the studio's new 6000-square-feet premises at 520 King Street West. A major custom printing job for Ruth Tulving early in 1972 had provided the $1000 cash needed to pay the first and last month's rent for the large, third-floor warehouse, which trebled the work space available to Open Studio.

Now, with sufficient space and increased equipment, Open Studio was clearly a home for serious printmakers. There would be no more thoughts of dressmaking classes. Instead, small, intensive classes in etching, lithography and screenprocess were organized to help finance the studio as well as spread the word about printmaking. Throughout its history Open Studio has emphasized the educational aspects of its program. To ensure consistently high technical standards, staff, artists renting facilities and students are continually involved in an exchange of skills and knowledge.

The rental program continued to be an important feature of Open Studio: the new King Street facilities provided space and equipment for a maximum of thirty-five artists to work cooperatively making prints. In recent years the studio space has always been filled, and most artists rent on a long-term basis.

Custom print jobs also began to increase after the move. In 1972 Open Studio produced sixteen custom editions, and in 1973 Joyce Wieland, James B. Spencer and other artists more than doubled that number, using the master-printer services of Sewell, Holman and Eugene Mazzei, who had replaced Hall as director of the etching department. The studio's own publishing program, initiated by Holman, also began in 1973, with several guest artists producing eighteen print editions in that year. In subsequent years the three area directors have continued to ask guest artists to join the publishing program, and in recent years Open Studio has begun to focus on publishing the work of its resident artists. Revenue from the sale of Open Studio prints has risen dramatically over the years.

By 1973 enough prints had already been produced to warrant the hiring of Jacquie Boughner as Open Studio's first curator. There are now more than 1500 works in the archives, which includes full documentation of all editions printed at the studio. All prints in the current exhibition have been selected from the Open Studio archives.

In 1973 Barbara Hall took a leave of absence. From that point she began to concentrate more on painting and returned to Open Studio only in the summers to work on editions of her prints. This was also the first year in which the Open Studio budget proposed the position of general manager as a separate job in the studio's organization. Sewell had been fulfilling this function, but needed to devote his time to his work as director of screenprocess. Kay Bridge was hired as general manager in January 1974, and in September Jini Stolk replaced her, with the new title of studio coordinator. Stolk continued in this capacity for the next six years.

Since salaries were still not financially feasible, a system of retainers was proposed in March 1974 to provide the staff with some sort of remuneration. These were a meagre $200 a month, projected to rise eventually to $300, and from these, deductions were made for unemployment insurance, workmen's compensation and income tax. The Open Studio staff was obviously working for love not money. In 1974-1975 arts council grants rose to a total of $47,252 ($25,252 from the Ontario Arts Council and $22,000 from the Canada Council), and Open Studio received its first grant from the Corporation of Metropolitan Toronto.

During the fall of 1974 William Kurelek came to the studio to work on a suite of four multicoloured lithographs with Don Holman. This was the period of Kurelek's greatest involvement with Open Studio. In December Jules Heller, the former dean of fine arts at York University, became associated with Open Studio for one year. No honorarium was offered with this consultant position, but Heller was given access to the staff and equipment at Open Studio to enable him to make editions of his own work.

In 1975 Open Studio's growing exhibition program went international. Stolk, the studio coordinator, and Pierre Boutin, head of visual arts at the Canadian Cultural Centre in Paris, France, organized a tour of thirty prints by eighteen Open Studio artists in Paris, London and Edinburgh.

Equipment is obviously a crucial ingredient in the success of a printmaking facility. From the first small press, Open Studio's principal equipment has grown to include a French tool press, a Praga press and a Sturges press in etching; two Praga presses and a wide variety of stones in lithography; and a large press, three small presses, five drying racks, two light tables and more than one hundred screens in screenprocess. Particularly important acquisitions along the way included the first set of viscosity rollers in etching in 1974. (The studio now has four of these sets.) Viscosity rollers, which allow colour work in etching, greatly extended the potential of the etching department. Capital equipment purchases projected for the next two years include a Charles Brand lithography press, a press in etching and a small vacuum printing table in screenprocess.

By mid-decade Open Studio was clearly healthy and growing, with facilities steadily improving and opportunities continually opening for a wide variety of artists who used them well and eagerly. As Open Studio flourished, the techniques and imaginations of the printmakers who worked there seemed to ripen too.

In 1975 Sewell requested a year's leave of absence. In September Brian Kelley was hired as director of etching, to take over from Mazzei, and Paul Feldman and Otis Tamasauskas joined the staff at the same time. Feldman replaced Sewell as director of screenprocess, and Tamasauskas shared the duties of director of lithography with Holman. These new hirings marked the beginning of a staff organization that continues to function today: a director and assistant director in each area. Also in 1975 Open Studio received two summer apprentices through the Ontario government's Experience '75 program. One of these workers, Elma Schumacher, was employed in October to fill the part-time position of studio curator. Open Studio continued to receive the services of two apprentices each summer until 1980, when cutbacks in government funding for the arts reduced the available apprenticeships to a single position.

In 1976 guest artists, including Vera Frankel, Kosso Eloul, Jack Bush and Mel Benson, continued to work with the master printers at Open Studio. In February of that year the board of directors made a commitment to repay the founding staff a small portion of the salaries lost in previous years because of insufficient funds. Payments of these "directors' loans" were made over the next four years.

In recent years there has been a dedicated and steady growth in all aspects of Open Studio operations. The volume of printmaking, the number of exhibitions, the extent of classes and the amount of grants continue to grow, despite the disturbing financial squeeze being felt by all art institutions in Canada today. Hundreds of artists have rented Open Studio facilities for the production of their own work, and hundreds of students have learned everything from the basics to the subtlest techniques in etching, screenprocess and lithography.

By 1977 Open Studio was clearly recognized as a major printmaking facility in Canada. The studio participated in the Canada

Council's Conference on Print workshops in Ottawa in March 1977, and during that year completed an edition for Gordon Smith and began a series of four editions with York Wilson. In September the studio welcomed its first international guest artist, Mexican printmaker Raymundo Sesma, who worked at Open Studio for eight months. His visit was arranged through the Department of External Affairs to coincide in part with Prime Minister Trudeau's trip to Mexico early in 1978. An exhibition of Open Studio prints also opened in Puebla, Puebla, Mexico at that time.

In 1977 the board of directors, which had been undergoing gradual changes in personnel through the years, decided that the Open Studio coordinator should join its ranks. Two years later one staff member and one member of the committee representing the artists renting Open Studio facilities were also added to the permanent board membership.

In the past two years Open Studio has begun to focus more on the publication of work by its own staff, and in 1978 *The Open Studio Book*, a bound portfolio of prints, was produced under the direction of Brian Kelley. A similar publication is slated for this year.

Some changes in staff occurred in 1979. Elma Schumacher left the post of curator in April and was replaced by Wendy Knox-Leet. Tamasauskas assumed responsibilities as director in etching, and Kelley became assistant director. In September Holman began a year's leave of absence and was replaced by Nick Novak, with Susan Farquhar filling the assistant director position in lithography. On the board of directors Yves Cousineau retired after seven years as president and J.F.W. Weatherill was named to head the board.

All the arts felt severe cutbacks in 1979. The Canada Council froze its maximum grant for print workshops at $30,000, the sum Open Studio was already receiving at that time. However, a special marketing and distribution grant from the Canada Council helped with the considerable finances the studio required. (By 1979 the Open Studio operating budget had reached $165,000.)

Early in 1979 Sewell added a new and important angle to the educational opportunities being offered by Open Studio. The Tutorial Editions Program (TEP) in screenprocess offers artists an in-depth, six-month work course aimed at providing them with the knowledge and skills to publish their own screenprocess edi-

tions. Important publishing and custom printing jobs continued to add to the reputation and revenues of Open Studio in 1979: Harold Klunder, Yves Gaucher, Reinhardt Reitzenstein and Louis de Niverville all produced work at the studio in that year. In June 1979, as in the summer before, Open Studio staff people conducted an etching workshop for artists from Sherbrooke, Quebec.

In 1980, the year marking the beginning of Open Studio's second decade of significant work in printmaking, many of the studio's activities related to the production of the current ten-year anniversary exhibition. In March Cyndra MacDowall was hired to supervise and coordinate all activities planned for the ten-year celebrations and exhibition. She became the first special project employee of the studio. Other staff changes during this year have included the retirement of Wendy Knox-Leet as curator in April and of Jini Stolk as studio coordinator in July. Orienda Caranci is the new curator, and Judith Stephens-Wells is coordinator.

Everyone involved with the remarkable maturing of Open Studio—staff, artist renters, guest artists, students and the board —possess a common concern for the art of printmaking, and by nurturing the openness and cooperation that have been crucial to Open Studio from the start, they will continue to find fruitful ways to keep Open Studio a strong and productive contributor to the lifeblood of Canadian art.

The studio and its significant creativity exist today primarily because of the vision, tenacity and art of the founders. To them and to the art of printmaking, Open Studio dedicates the next decade.

The following programs are of special significance to the unique character of Open Studio.

EDUCATIONAL PROGRAMS
The educational thrust of Open Studio is twofold. On the one hand, there is a program for the instruction of amateurs from the general public; on the other, there is the instruction of professional artists and printmakers who work in the studio on a regular basis. This latter form of education takes place in depth and aims at the highest standards, for the quality of the studio's print production depends upon it.

The public education program seeks to raise the appreciation, technical skills and general knowledge of a wide variety of people interested in printmaking. It includes:

1. Classes. Small classes of five to six students meet for two and a half hours, three nights a week for a total of four weeks. These classes are taught by artists who are also trained printers in etching, lithography and screenprocess. Each student works independently, according to his or her ability.

2. Workshops. Over the years Open Studio has given a variety of workshops consisting of one, two or three-day sessions on photo techniques in screenprocess and etching and techniques in collotype. Workshops have been offered in other locations, including the St. Michael's Printshop in Newfoundland; Moosonee, Ontario; Red Lake, Manitoba; and several other cities.

3. Lecture–demonstrations. These have been delivered before a wide variety of audiences, including collectors, dealers and gatherings at museums and galleries.

4. Tours. Forty to fifty groups tour Open Studio each year to watch printmakers at work.

Because the studio is intended to function primarily as a production facility for original prints, there is an ongoing educational program for the professional. At the centre of this informal program is the relationship between the master printer and the apprentice helper who assists him or her for many months, slowly acquiring the range of skills and attitudes needed to produce work of the highest quality. The apprentice helpers are drawn mainly from the ranks of the artists renting Open Studio facilities.

While the apprenticeship program is used to teach both etching and screenprocess, it is particularly suited to lithography, where logistics of the technique often require two people to share the responsibilities of the work. In all three areas apprentices work with master printers to produce each other's editions, as well as editions being printed in the custom printing program and works being published by the studio. It is not unusual for three or four apprentices to help produce a single edition.

Such give and take—knowledge in exchange for labour—lies at the heart of Open Studio's success. Using this principle, Richard Sewell recently developed the Tutorial Editions Program, which offers an intensive, six-month course designed to train printmakers to produce their own screenprocess editions.

EXHIBITIONS

Over the years Open Studio has mounted many exhibitions of prints and sent them to public and commercial galleries, universities and other locations, large and small, in North America and Europe. These exhibitions not only introduce Open Studio artists to the public, but also serve to illustrate various printmaking techniques.

The earliest exhibitions were informal affairs. Completed prints and works in progress were hung on the walls of the original Queen Street West studio, where they could be studied by both working artists and interested outsiders. Today this informal exhibiting is still carried on at the King Street West premises.

The studio's first formal exhibition was held in December 1971 in the Edward Johnson Building at the University of Toronto. This show included eighty prints by twenty-three artists associated with the studio. Among the participants were Judy Gouin, Barbara Hall, Nikolette Jakovac, Richard Sewell, John Street, Francesca Vivenza and Joy Walker.

During the next nine years the exhibition program expanded rapidly through the initiative of Open Studio staff and guest artists. In 1975 Jini Stolk, studio coordinator, and Pierre Boutin, head of visual arts at the Canadian Cultural Centre in Paris, France, organized an international tour of thirty prints by eighteen Open Studio artists. This international exhibition received favourable reviews when it appeared at Canada House in London, England; the Talbot Rice Centre in Edinburgh, Scotland; and the Cultural Centre in Paris. Europeans seemed amazed that this kind of cooperative printmaking facility existed at all, let alone produced such high-quality work.

In September 1975 Open Studio exhibited thirty-seven prints at the Glenbow-Alberta Institute in Calgary, and three years later thirty-five prints were shown at Culture House in Puebla, Puebla, Mexico.

The growth of the exhibition program has been assisted by Open Studio's association with the Art Gallery of Ontario Extension Services, which has circulated two shows of Open Studio prints. In 1973-1974 one show toured seven Ontario exhibition centres, and in 1975-1977 a second show visited fourteen centres in the province. The Art Gallery of Ontario Extension Services will circulate the current exhibition, *Open Studio: Ten Years*, throughout 1981 and 1982.

A partial list of Open Studio exhibitions in the first ten years includes:

1971
Edward Johnson Building, University of Toronto

1973
Bowmanville Art Gallery
Glendon College, York University
Morris Gallery, Toronto

1973-1974
Art Gallery of Ontario Extension Services tour

1974
Guelph University
Glendon College, York University

1975
City Hall, Toronto
Glenbow-Alberta Institute, Calgary
Princess Margaret Lodge, Toronto
Pollock Gallery, Toronto

1975-1976
International tour to London, Edinburgh and Paris

1975-1977
Art Gallery of Ontario Extension Services tour

1976
Macdonald Block, Queen's Park, Toronto
Agnes Etherington Arts Centre, Kingston, Ont.

1977
Arts & Letters Club, Toronto
Fleet Galleries, Winnipeg
Heliconian Club, Toronto
Seneca College, Toronto

Scott McKennis Gallery, Norfolk, Va.
Old Dominion University, Norfolk, Va.

1978
Culture House, Puebla, Puebla, Mexico
Eaton's Art Gallery, Toronto
Gallery Graphics, Ottawa
St. Lawrence College Gallery, Kingston, Ont.

1979
Albright-Knox Art Gallery (Members Gallery), Buffalo, N.Y.

1980
McMaster University, Hamilton, Ont.
The Art Gallery at Harbourfront, Toronto, Ont.

VISITING ARTISTS AND THE PUBLISHING PROGRAM
Open Studio's publishing program has placed original prints by Canadian artists in public and private collections throughout the world. The program originated in 1973, when Don Holman, director of lithography, contacted several well-known artists who were not primarily printmakers, but whose work was respected and who had expressed interest in the printing media. In the first year of the program Open Studio published editions by Kim Andrews, Alex Cameron, Barbara Hall, Walt Humphries, Hans Schweizer, James B. Spencer and Richard Sewell. Open Studio has continued to invite outside artists to work with the studio staff and facilities. These artists fall into four categories:

1. Invited by one of the three area directors. (This type of invitation was generally extended in the early days of the studio before operations became organized enough for the staff to sit down and discuss a list of prospective visiting artists.)
2. Invited by Open Studio.
3. Invited jointly by Open Studio and the Canada Council Art Bank.
4. Invited under sponsorship of other organizations, such as art schools and government departments. (Johann Feucht, a student from the Alberta College of Art, is working at Open Studio

this year, and Raymundo Sesma, Open Studio's first international visiting artist, was brought from Mexico under the auspices of the Department of External Affairs.)

Under the visiting artist program the master printer and guest artist donate their time and skills to a given project. Open Studio supplies the use of its equipment and the necessary materials. Upon completion of the edition, the prints are priced according to the cost of the edition, the donated labour and the market value of the artist's work. These editions are usually marketed by Open Studio. The studio and the artist share in the proceeds of the sales, the studio recovering its investment at cost and the remainder being shared between the studio and the artist.

In 1976 Imperial Oil and Norcen Energy Resources sponsored such a partnership between artist and master printer when they helped finance the publishing of an edition by Kosso Eloul, produced under the direction of Richard Sewell. Other work published at Open Studio by guest artists included an edition by Gordon Smith in 1977 and editions by Rita Letendre and Michael Poulton in 1978.

In 1979 the studio began to publish works by some of its own staff and by some of the artists involved in the rental plan, including Sandra Altwerger, Don Holman, Elma Schumacher, Louise Zurosky, Brian Kelley, Robert Game, Lorna Livey and Otis Tamasauskas. In the same year Harold Klunder participated in the publication of a print, *Elderslie*, in which master printer Nick Novak worked with the artist to produce an edition of extraordinary beauty.

Publishing provides exciting opportunities for the fruitful interaction of artists and printers, and planning is now underway to ensure the continuation and growth of this program in the 1980s. At present, Open Studio is finalizing an arrangement under the Twin Cities program between Toronto and Amsterdam, Holland, which will send a studio artist to work in Amsterdam as a guest of the Dutch government in 1980-1981.

Open Studio Founders
Richard Sewell
Barbara Hall
Don Holman

Founding Board of Directors
Yves Cousineau, president
Ruth Tulving, vice-president
Gayle Goldberg, vice-president
Eugene Tellez, vice-president
Hamilton Cassels Jr., secretary

Current Board of Directors, 1979-1980
J.F.W. Weatherill, president
Robert White, treasurer
Hamilton Cassels Jr., secretary
Lyman Henderson, vice-president (retired 1980)
Elsie Agnew, vice-president
Brian Kelley, director of etching, Open Studio
Robert Game, artist
Larry Donaldson, Artist Renters Committee representative

Staff
Jini Stolk, coordinator (retired 1980)
Judith Stephens-Wells, coordinator
Orienda Caranci, administrative assistant

ETCHING DEPARTMENT
Brian Kelley
Otis Tamasauskas

SCREENPROCESS DEPARTMENT
Richard Sewell
Paul Feldman

LITHOGRAPHY DEPARTMENT
Don Holman
Nick Novak
Susan Farquhar

Nikolette Jakovac, *Dry Tangerines*

OPEN STUDIO AND PRINTMAKING: A BRIEF HISTORY

For an opinion on the importance of being ten, one should go not to a senior citizen but to the celebrant of this benchmark in the slow journey from seed to full achievement. At ten one is beginning to be conscious of self, to have the first clear intimations of ambition, to have enough sense of time to say "Long ago when I was very young", to be competitive and proud of the signs of progress, but also aware of one's frailties and vulnerabilities. The associates of Open Studio are right to feel entitled to some notice for having survived and for having achieved a real degree of distinction in an endeavour for which no such success could have been foreseen.

THE BEGINNINGS OF OPEN STUDIO

A cooperative is neither a person nor an institution. It cannot relax in the comfort of a statistically reasonable life expectancy. It cannot dream of the centuries society may allow universities and other useful or uplifting and entertaining public enterprises, such as state theatres and museums. When a cooperative is composed of artists, who are the archetypal individualists of modern times, its chances of survival beyond a season or two seem very slight. Artists seldom embark on long-range projects except out of desperation or idealism or some combination of these contradictory emotions. The one impulse is generated by learning the hard way that some very worthwhile things cannot be done alone, the other by the generous feeling that benefits ought to be shared.

The desperation, as in the case of the founders of Open Studio, usually precedes the idealism. The initial vision is apt to be unclear and faltering. Purpose, form and mechanics take shape out of experience.

As so often is the case with the formative experiences of youth, the story of Open Studio began almost spontaneously, without any plan or idea where it might lead. What is remarkable about it is that with some considerable precocity a design did begin to be perceptible and a reasoned program for development was followed. These lines are being written because the enterprise has reached a stage where its participants have begun to make a series of connected observations about their achievement and to ask some pertinent questions beyond the obvious one of what is likely to happen next. They have thought that sharing their history might help other artists with similar problems. And they have become curious, in a spirit not of exaggerated self-pride but of increasing professional maturity, to know how their efforts look in the context of the history of printmaking. This essay is my attempt, at their request, to answer this question.

The name Open Studio was adopted to express the founders' central aim: to be an unaffiliated workshop under professional direction, prepared to do high-quality graphic printing on a contract basis as a part of its support, but also open to artists who might, for a fee, do their own work with proper equipment or receive technical instruction in a professional atmosphere. At the time, the only remotely similar opportunities for printmaking in Canada were the professional closed shop at the Nova Scotia School of Art and Design in Halifax and Richard Lacroix's Guilde Graphique and Pierre Ayot's Graff in Montreal. That something more was badly needed is shown by the fact that during the past decade twelve more printmaking facilities have appeared on the scene, at least two as direct offshoots of Open Studio. Why this should have happened in Canada cannot be properly explained unless we examine, if too briefly, some ancient history in Europe and some more recent history in the United States.

THE BEGINNINGS OF EUROPEAN PRINTMAKING

To begin with, it is a common misapprehension that great printmakers—Dürer, Rembrandt, Goya, Picasso—appeared spontaneously like comets in the sky. There may also be those who imagine either that printmaking, like embalming, was a discovery of the ancient Egyptians or that it was invented by Andy Warhol.

The notion that an image could not only be created but could also be multiplied by transferring and cutting it into a piece of metal or wood and then pressing it in reverse onto paper with ink came surprisingly late in the history of art. This is truly astonishing when one considers that systems for reproducing patterns by impressing in clay or on cloth with die or roller were developed in many early civilizations, including some pre-literate ones.

It is extraordinary that during the four thousand years of pre-Gutenberg book making, from the scriptoria of the Egyptian Old Kingdom to those of late medieval monasteries and the earlier Medici, it never occurred to anyone that there was an easier way to duplicate a manuscript than by laborious copying, letter by letter and line by line—a process that increased the available number only by a single copy, not by one hundred or one hundred thousand. The idea of an edition of a book or image, with or without limits, was inconceivable before the appearance of movable type and the development of presses capable of dealing with the new requirements and potentials of this invention. This applied as much to the individual, single-printed sheet as to whole books, illustrated or not, and the heavier presses required for the latter became necessary not long after the introduction of broadsides printed from single blocks.

From the very beginning printing was associated with the idea of purpose. The question of utility or purpose is in itself quite fascinating. Most of the energy devoted to the single-sheet woodcuts or metal prints that were turned out in some quantity on the eve of Gutenberg's important invention was given to the production of devotional images. This is just what we ought to expect from the twilight of the medieval era. The lord or rich merchant could and would go on as before commissioning an artist to paint a splendid altarpiece, but now, suddenly the man or woman with pennies to spend rather than ducats could buy a nice devotional woodcut of the Madonna or the Crucifixion to pin over the fireplace, exactly as we see in many old paintings.

Some of these fragile and apparently ephemeral things have managed to survive because they were pasted into the undecorated ends of early books or inside the lids of travelling chests. Here the prints might have had an apotropaic intention, to avert by their very presence theft or other hazards of travel. They could turn the chest into a portable altar as well, and they also filled the practical purpose of keeping dust from sifting through the cracks.

These early devotional prints served an audience by no means confined to the relatively poor. And at the very same time another form of print was being sold to the idle rich just under the level of those who could afford to employ court painters: this was the sets of elegant playing cards, especially the elaborate tarots that are once again fashionable.

In both cases—holy images or the counters of worldly games—the pieces that have come down to us tell us something else: prints in their fifteenth-century infancy were either black on white or the reverse. We see that at least as early as when Mrs. Dürer was sent on the road to broaden the market for her hus-

band's prints, the children of artist-printers were put to work colouring prints in order to extend the base of household employment to its maximum. They could give the Virgin a blue robe, place little yellow stars in her heaven or put green trees in the landscape purporting to show Jerusalem.

The development of printing was important for reasons almost impossible for us to imagine in our world, where the art print is a luxury item addressed to special audiences and where mechanically reproduced images appear in millions of copies of newspapers and magazines and are made instantly, if fleetingly, visible on countless television screens. To have dared predict anything resembling such miracles in the century or two after Gutenberg in Nürnberg or Antwerp, Venice or Paris—all places where intense artistic activity was accomplished in an atmosphere charged with both superstition and hard-nosed practicality—would have won a quick ticket to the chambers of the Inquisition. But we must try to understand this older world view if we are to comprehend the central role that printmaking held in that world and would continue to hold until modern times, when the advent of mechanical means for proliferating images pushed handmade articles into the realm of the nonessential.

In its early days printing was used primarily for instruction, and the concept of "art for art's sake" had not arisen. One cannot, however, deny that a picture not only made education more easily and fully understood but also made the process far more attractive. The engraver's art was essential to the dissemination of information in the then burgeoning fields of scientific and intellectual experimentation. It is staggering to realize the range of areas in which this was true, all the way from agronomy, anatomy, archery and astrology to zoology. Problems in mathematics and engineering were made clear by engraved diagrams; history and even law were made more palatable reading by illustrations. The contributions of the artist-engraver to the knowledge of the physical world, as conveyed, for example, by atlases and florilegia, are beyond calculation and are hardly the worse for the fact that these artists long regarded truth to be inseparable from the charms of imaginative interpretation or even sheer embellishment. Knowledge of human anatomy was furthered through the superb prints of Mantegna, Pollaiuolo, Dürer and those assistants of Titian generally given credit for the seminal illustrations to Vesalius.

For a time the early engravers were content to go on working productively with book publishers, adding to and improving their techniques, easily selling their separate prints at local shops and the big international fairs. They worked in an exclusionist world in which independent practice depended on certification of competence through the guilds (submission of the "master-work" as proof) and the fine arts were merely subsections of broader guilds, such as those of physicians and goldsmiths.

This system was operating smoothly when the artists themselves introduced two new factors. They became aware of the power of advertising, for which the print was an admirable and cheap international vehicle, and the best or vainest among them decided to demand a distinct, unprecedented and high social status. They engraved or had their assistants engrave small reproductions of masterpieces that were not transportable, and they began to demand rewards and recognition that would disassociate them forever from their traditional and more or less menial place among artisans. Though they continued to work with their hands, they now insisted that the source of their powers lay in brain and soul; in other words, it wasn't how but what and why that counted. Raphael and Michelangelo led the march, presently joined by Titian. At this precise time a schism began in printmaking that has never disappeared. Unfortunately, it began to be thought that either a great print had to be made by a great artist or else it was a mere reflection turned out by a journeyman.

Beginning in about 1470, cycles of notable printmaking production occurred at first at intervals of about fifty years and then accelerated to a tempo closer to every thirty years. Why these cycles recur at regular intervals is not clear. However, it is clear that the epicentres for European printmaking have always tended to be cities where flourishing book-production industries coincided with the presence of exceptional clusters of gifted artists: Nürnberg and Basel, Venice and Florence, Paris, Antwerp, Amsterdam and, ultimately, London. This seems to be only partially true in Canada and the United States, which may be because in Europe there has been a persistent tradition of compatibility between artists and writers that is most uncommon in North America.

The most important and, in fact, archetypal phenomenon in the history of international printmaking in its second generation (and one of the best illustrations of its cyclical character) arose from the decision of the French king François I to import a large and distinguished team of Italian artists, mostly recruited in Mantua, to decorate the rapidly expanding palace at Fontainebleau. About ten years after the work began, these painters, sculptors and virtuoso plaster-workers suddenly developed, almost as a pastime, an intense interest in the arts of etching and engraving, the execution of which they delegated to their assistants. They experimented with techniques, papers and coloured inks. They expanded the range of subject matter, which had less and less to do with piety and even included pornography. This fever of creative activity lasted a scant six years from 1542, but its repercussions were to be felt in recurrent waves through the next three-quarters of a century, during the phases of the stylistic movement now called Mannerism.

The advanced craft of these artists was soon profitably vulgarized by the printing industry in Paris. Their works, sent all over northern Europe as propaganda for the splendour and power of the French court, spread at the same time the doctrines of an avantgarde style. These artists were continually being rediscovered, and their profound influence on printmaking was felt not only in the traditional printing strongholds, but also in Nancy, Frankfurt and Prague. Unlike most other movements, this one inspired remarkable artists who were mainly, if not solely, printmakers, such as Duvet, Beatrizet, Bellange and Spranger. Callot and Hollar were late heirs to this tradition, and the young Rembrandt drew on its lessons. In all this, the principal carrier was style, not process.

An example of a great revolution brought about by the invention of a new medium or process is that of lithography. It is an ironic history, for Senefelder's discovery in the last days of the eighteenth century had nothing to do with art, let alone revolution. He and his friends saw lithography as a way to speed up the output and reduce the cost of printing sheet music. A few English artists, including John Crome, saw the artistic potential of this development almost at once, but for the next twenty years in Paris lithography was taken up mainly by amateurs as a sort of parlour accomplishment. But when finally realized, its expressive possibilities must have sounded like drumrolls to young rebels such as Géricault and Delacroix. The appeal of lithography to the young Romantics put the new process on the artistic map, and there it has remained, though again with an undulating history of periods of relative neglect followed by strong revivals in the hands of new generations with fresh approaches.

These revivals of interest in the graphic arts (not only lithography) from the mid nineteenth century onward have often witnessed short-lived associations of artists intent on increasing public interest in their endeavours. However, in Europe the effectiveness of those artists' societies was almost invariably secondary to the impact of printer-publishers, such as Ambroise Vollard.

PRINTMAKING IN THE UNITED STATES

The North American story is different. For most of the nineteenth century, graphic art on this continent tended not to attract the best available talent. In both the United States and Canada many prints were designed either to rouse European interest in our constantly expanding frontier real estate, with its apparently endless stock of natural wonders, or to satisfy curiosity about the life of the American people, especially the Indians. The famous New York lithography firm, Currier & Ives, lithographed 4300 subjects between 1835 and 1907 and marketed them throughout America and western Europe. The company's professional lithographers copied a wide variety of paintings, commissioned sketches and prints, but did not allow painters to draw their own designs on stone.

The American Civil War sparked an age of illustrated magazines at a time when wood engraving and steel engraving were the main processes, but apart from Winslow Homer's work there is little memorable in this period. Fortunately for the United States, Whistler and Mary Cassatt were respected participants in the great graphic revivals in Paris in the 1860s and at the end of the century. Though both these artists settled permanently abroad, their influences were strongly felt in North America. In London another American, Joseph Pennell, proved to be a great influence on both artists and print connoisseurs in the late nineteenth century.

In the first decades of our century the group of artists known as The Eight — eventually called the Ashcan Painters — proved enthusiastic printmakers. These artists, including William Glackens, Robert Henri and John Sloan, inspired occasional followers in New York and Philadelphia who, like themselves, expressed a distinctly American flavour in their work. But whenever a distinctive personality appeared in American printmaking between the wars, the presence of Paris was almost invariably felt. And often in the second decade of that period, in the 1930s, the persuasive influence was that of Stanley Hayter's Atelier 17. His influence continued still more directly when he and the workshop moved to New York as war refugees in 1941. Here is surely a close ancestor of Open Studio.

The regionalism of the 1930s provoked a small wave of activity among artists who found prints more saleable than oils during the Depression. In an effort to throw a lifeline to artists all but starving on Works Projects Administration grants, the San Francisco *Chronicle* commissioned about forty of them each to produce a limited-edition lithograph. These, printed on good paper on an old *Chronicle* hand press, were given splendid publicity and made available to subscribers at a dollar or so a sheet. What might have been a West Coast renaissance was arrested by the war.

Major American museums after 1900 built magnificent print departments, but by focussing on the Old Masters (William Blake often marked the dividing line), their influence was clearly stronger on collectors than on artists. American printmakers had to wait for the foundation of the Museum of Modern Art and the inauguration of the Brooklyn Museum's splendidly serious graphic biennials for their cause to be taken up and their merits sorted out. Other museums, notably in Chicago, San Francisco, Philadelphia and Washington, picked up this important mission. Specialist dealers began to appear not long after the war, and when the artists were ready to join a really big wave of print enthusiasm, most of the American support system was already in place.

World War II marks the gulf between the adopted traditions of almost five hundred years of printing and the beginning of new systems of support and training for American printmakers. Art education began to be taken over by universities, and there im-

Moira Clark, *Full Moonlight*

mediately emerged an exceptionally influential school of graphic art at the University of Iowa, under the direction of Maurice Lazansky. At least one of the early graduate students was Canadian: Roloff Beny was singled out for praise for daring mixed-media experiments in 1946. The range of printmaking possibilities was soon expanded by an increased accessibility of silkscreen process.

But a few conscientious printmakers were already aware of a problem that has since become endemic: college-trained printmakers had learned at least the rudiments of techniques, but were left quite innocent of ideas about professional procedures and standards as they tried to embark on independent careers.

A few women artists, who began to show their constructive concern in the first years of the 1950s, proved to be the main catalysts for dealing with the various problems plaguing American printmaking at that time. June Wayne was already vocalizing her concerns in California in 1952. Far more artist and practical philosopher than entrepreneur, Wayne thought that these problems lay in four areas: the all but total absence in America of master printers and centres where artists could find the best equipment and technical help; the need for full documentation; the lack of recognized business and artistic ethics and standards; and the need to educate artists, collectors, curators and dealers in these matters. She set about energetically solving these problems, studying the great ateliers in Paris and persuading three master printers there to come to California long enough to train other printers. Wayne then got the Ford Foundation to underwrite a considerable share of the high costs for this nursery period, which included building a superbly designed and equipped lithography centre and setting up this facility as a foundation where mature artists with a need for printing help or a desire to improve their skills could come to work for set periods with bursaries.

Direct merchandising was avoided, but the dealers soon began to ring the bell. The rest is history, with the flourishing of the Tamarind Press; the training and stimulating of master printers, such as Ken Tyler of the Gemini Press, who set up other centres; and the ultimate transfer of Tamarind to the University of New Mexico, where it continues its distinguished career. The professional ideals worked out in that unlikely setting just off Holly-wood Boulevard were to find a worthy spiritual descendant in Toronto.

Meanwhile, on the East Coast a new generation of New York artists, including Jasper Johns, Robert Rauschenberg, Helen Frankenthaler and Jim Dine, was rediscovering the print as a challenging medium full of potential for radical innovation. These artists found a special haven at Universal Limited Art Editions, the highly professional, adventurous, production-geared and promotionally knowledgeable graphic-printing centre being developed on Long Island by a Russian emigré artist, Tatyana Grosman. Grosman's extraordinary gift for spotting talent and her great shrewdness and obvious probity transformed this experimental operation into a high-quality, high-profit closed-shop production line, a sort of Rolls Royce factory of the print world.

OPEN STUDIO AND CANADIAN PRINTMAKING

This is the moment for us to return to Canada and to ask what sort of situation faced Open Studio's founders. The graphic media have always had a few practitioners in this country, but there has been no continuous history, no line of consistent development, no tradition and, until very recently, neither any committed printmakers of real distinction nor any pool of collector-patrons. Dealers were, with the rarest exceptions, almost totally disinterested in prints, carried them only as a sideline and preferred to show modern European and American artists. In the late 1960s and early 1970s Toronto saw the quick demise of several optimistic efforts to launch galleries devoted exclusively to graphic art. Whether the prints were old or new seemed to make no difference. (One notable exception to this situation was the Pascal Gallery in Toronto, which dealt exclusively in prints.) Museums offered little or no support. There were societies of graphic artists, but even under the leadership of such enthusiastic transplants as Nicholas Hornyansky, they never rose out of the shadow of the stronger societies of painters or managed to move perceptibly out of the rearguard.

It is not worth examining in detail the reasons for this state of affairs. I suspect the influence of working situations at Grip prejudiced the Group of Seven and their successors against the graphic media in a period when these meant mainly scratchboard illustrations for magazines and homegrown books or, in prephotoprocess days, the engravings for Eaton's catalogues. Between the wars Dorothy Stevens managed to make a more than local name as an etcher, but the general picture in that period is bleak. However, after World War II the work of Toronto lithographer Jack Nichols became well known, though Nichols had to make several trips to Paris to practice his art because of the virtual absence of lithographic facilities in Canada. In fact, there cannot have been much available in the way of proper equipment in any of the printmaking media except for the occasional small studio press.

I described the situation of the Open Studio founders in 1970 as being close to desperate. But the gods were clearly on their side. The timing of their efforts coincided with the beginnings of an extended period of good printmaking. In the past decade the print has become a major mode of expression everywhere, as we experience one of those cyclical peaks in the history of graphic media. In Canada prints have attracted the interest of many of our best artists and have won wide esteem among younger collectors. The print has engaged or enlarged the support of some of our most serious dealers, now proud to feature Canadian work. Museum attitudes have changed: the Art Gallery of Ontario has added a curatorial department for prints and drawings, allotted excellent space for study and storage, allocated purchase funds and organized print shows for circulation. The increase in the number of serious art-printing centres in Canada from two to twelve is another significant indicator of the thrust the 1970s gave to printmaking. Whether success spurs emulation or differences of opinion is not for me to say, but by some process of benign fission Open Studio has at this precocious age already produced several offshoots, notably Don Phillip's Sword Street Press. Of course, as the popularity of printmaking increases, so does the demand for available funds and facilities.

This is not the place for a critical appraisal of the work on exhibition. But for what they say about the existence and conduct of Open Studio, several summary observations are appropriate. Between them the three printmaking departments at Open Studio have risen over the past decade to a production tempo of three and a half editions per week, obviously much higher now than at the outset and, incidentally, generating about half the studio's operating costs. The juried selection for this exhibition has been drawn from a total of 1500 editions produced up to February 1980. Of the major Canadian artists who have interested themselves in the graphic arts, almost all have worked with Open Studio. However, many of the names in the current exhibition will be unfamiliar to the general public. But regardless of whether they are famous or relatively unknown, all the Open Studio artists have helped contribute to the genuine openness and high quality of this printmaking facility.

The solid level of performance found at Open Studio doesn't happen simply out of enthusiasm. It depends upon extreme devotion to both the art and the science of the graphic media; a high regard for technical quality; absolute probity; openness of mind as well as of facilities; sensitivity to each other and to the needs of clients; a balanced appreciation for the merits of both experiment and tradition; and a sense of responsibility toward good management, good housekeeping and toward the curatorial chores of documentation and maintaining in pristine condition the complete record collection of artists' proofs. All of these play their roles in the day-to-day activities of Open Studio printmakers. Their special duty toward the young artist has been observed with scrupulous care. They have earned the confidence of other established artists and art publishers, expressed by the steady volume of custom printing. They have won and kept many helpful friends in the community at large, including Jules Heller when he was dean of fine arts at York University, and they have been enormously helped by a small, committed and hard-working lay board.

These are more than impressive accomplishments for a ten-year-old. And what, above all, makes this enterprise shine in a very special way is Open Studio's unique combination of openness and professionalism. The literally open door of Open Studio is a humble but tremendously significant symbol. May the decade that door has been ajar continue in the same spirit, for here is a cooperative undertaking that has not only given satisfaction to its associates but also become a remarkable benefactor to the art life of a whole country.

Theodore Allen Heinrich
Professor of Visual Arts
York University

PERENNIAL FLOWERINGS

A decade ago a small but hardy cultural seed was sown in Toronto. A small group of enthusiastic young artist-printers (Richard Sewell, Barbara Hall and, later, Don Holman) opened a "shop-front" printing studio at 310 Queen Street West. In this unpromising environment, in an unfashionable area (at that time) they—with secondhand equipment and amateur students with intensely professional aspirations—set up a shop in which the artist could make his or her own prints in Toronto.

The years have gone by, and each year has seen a seasonal rebirth and perennial flowering as the small plant wintered over each financial year. The tender seedling was transplanted; the personnel nurturing each year's new growth has changed and been added to. Pruning and force-feeding with healthy funding has transformed this shabby little storefront into a warehouse professional printshop producing top-quality images of Canadian art in prints.

This hardy wintering over took place in an era of extravagances —frivolous enterprises, which rendered a future generation bankrupt. However, because of the perennial flowering of this modest planting the vaults of museums to be may well house the priceless printed images recording art of this time.

I doubt that the founders of Open Studio will be immortalized. I doubt that even the present studio staff is cognizant of how it all happened and from where and whence came this inheritance. I like to think, however, that every print that leaves this studio in the next decade will bear a tiny invisible imprint from each artist's thumb, guided by invisible hands that made a dream come true. And that in one hundred years or so some eager student will gain a Ph.D. for researching a history of the cultural climate of the 1970s and 1980s and find that modest beginnings with high aspirational intents were also possible in those years of Canadian extravagances.

In wishing a happy birthday to Open Studio, one can only wish and wait for an equally significant coming of age in another decade or so.

Anita Aarons
Director, The Art Gallery at Harbourfront

STATEMENT FROM THE SELECTION COMMITTEE

On reflection, the task of selecting an exhibition to represent Open Studio's activities over their first ten years was both stimulating and challenging. It was a pleasure to work on the Selection Committee with Judy Gouin and Glenda Milrod. From the outset our goal was to select work of the highest quality. The many hours of stimulating discussions, demanding reviews and interesting disagreements necessary to achieve the final selection left me satisfied about the level of commitment involved. Otis Tamasauskas, our technical advisor, provided incisive and thoughtful information, which I found to be a helpful aid in decision making. Above all, I found it rewarding to have the opportunity to look at the work of artists from this vital association, and I trust that the variety of approaches, styles and subjects in the exhibition will be enthusiastically scrutinized by the viewer.

Andrew Oko

Members of the Selection Committee
Andrew Oko, Curator, The Art Gallery of Hamilton
Glenda Milrod, Exhibition Producer, Art Gallery of Ontario
    Extension Services
Judy Gouin, Printmaker, Open Studio

Technical Advisor
Otis Tamasauskas, Printmaker, Open Studio

OPEN STUDIO: TEN YEARS

Sandra Altwerger, *Wild Iris*

Sandra Altwerger, *Barbados Canefield*

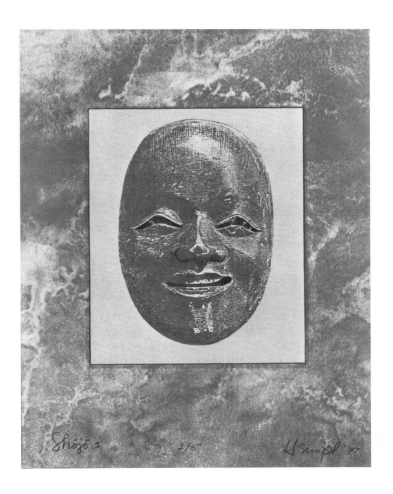

Hans Schweizer, *(Charlotte)*

Carol Heimpel, *Shojo I*

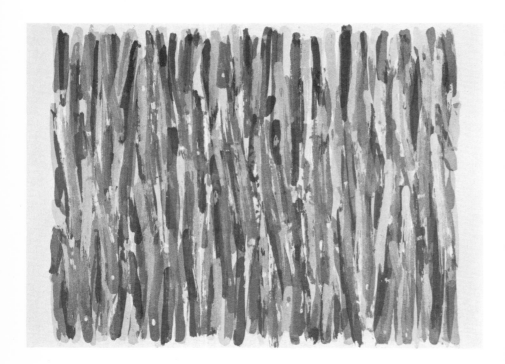

Joy Walker, untitled

Eugene Mazzei, untitled

Louis de Niverville, *Moonlighting*   Nikolette Jakovac, *Garden*

Lorna Livey, *Elmira Parlour Couch*

Brian Kelley, *The James River, Va.*

Elizabeth Hague, *The Park Entrance 2nd Version*

Elizabeth Hague, *Undine*

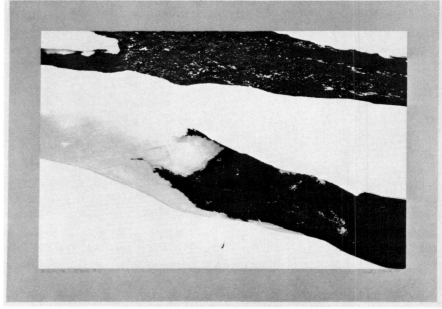

Judy Gouin, *Stumps*

Judy Gouin, *December Ice*

Peeled apple 05 Proof 1   Kelley

Brian Kelley, *Peeled Apple*

Open Studio Proof   Day Glow

Moira Clark, *Day Glow*

Judy Gouin, *Trees in Meadow*

Sandra Altwerger, *Beaver Slide*

Jan Winton, *Syncopation*

Barbara Hall, *Oasis*

Don Holman, *Southern Ontario*

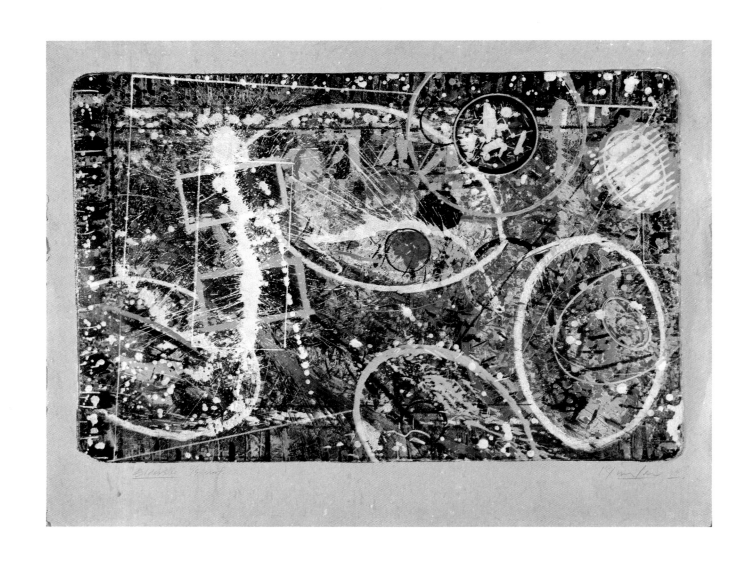

Harold Klunder, *Elderslie*

Otis Tamasauskas, *Japan Fan No. 6*

Richard Sewell, *Stopwatch*

Rita Letendre, *Orani*

Yves Gaucher, *Jericho/An Allusion to Barnett Newman*

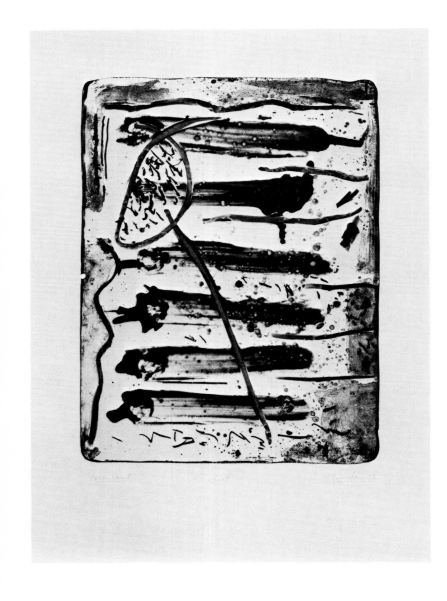

Harold Klunder, *Ivory Coast*   John Lander, *Coloured Dog Fish*

Erica Rutherford, *Still Life with Red*

Don Carr, *U.F.O.*

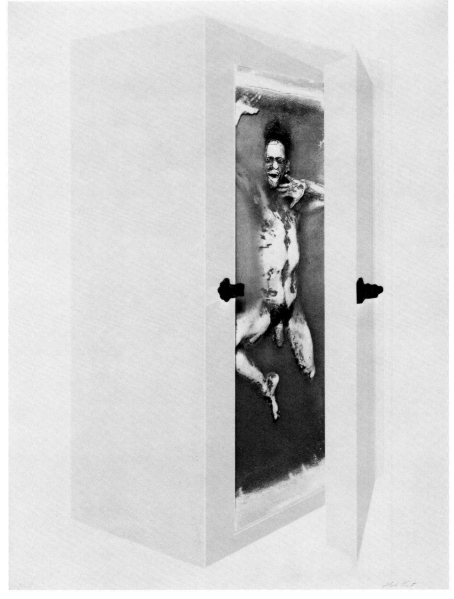

Mel Benson, *Our Elder*   Mark Prent, untitled

Denise Job, *Phases of the Heart*   James B. Spencer, *Reverse Wave*

Richard Sewell, *Starbuck/Sewell Suite I Blue*

Richard Sewell, *Starbuck/Sewell Suite II Pink*

Otis Tamasauskas, *Horn*

Jacques Benoît, *Diagonal*

The problem of defining exactly what a print is and of distinguishing between an "original print" and a "reproduction" is a source of ongoing debate in the art world. The following comments by printmakers at Open Studio are attempts to shed expert light on an area where there are many acceptable statements but no accepted definitions.

Original Print or Reproduction?

Categorical answers are usually given to the questions what is an original print? and what is a reproduction?

The "original print" is produced by hand. The image is hand drawn by the artist directly on the plates, stones or screens to be used in the printing. The inks are hand mixed, and the paper is handmade. The edition is also printed by hand, either by a printer or, in the case of a "printmaker", by the artist himself. Aesthetic decisions made during the process are made by the artist.

The "reproduction" is described as a print whose image is not hand drawn by the artist, but is copied photomechanically from an already existent drawing or painting. The reproduction is printed on some type of automated press, and there is no certainty that aesthetic decisions required during the printing were made by the artist. Decisions may have been made by technicians or printers using the photographed drawing or painting as a guide. In the case of "fine reproductions" there is usually a statement about the artist being the final arbiter in all aesthetic decisions.

These standard definitions imply that there are techniques for making original prints that are different and distinct from the techniques used for making reproductions. They also suggest that the process for making an original print is a non-photographic process, and the process for making a reproduction is a photomechanical one. But the ability to make a reproduction did not begin with the invention of photographic printing techniques.

The first photographically produced print was made in 1841. It was a Daguerreotype that was etched like an aquatint. This was printed as the first photomechanical reproduction in the Parisian magazine, *Excursions Daguerriennes*. The image was the Virgin's Funeral, a relief on Notre Dame Cathedral in Paris.

But almost four hundred years before the etched Daguerreotype we find both the ability to make a reproduction and, more importantly, the intent to make one. Johann Fust and Peter Schoeffer, the financiers of Gutenberg's experiments in movable type, not only published the famous Bible but also a series of Psalters.

Published in 1457, the book featured a specially created typeface based on stylizations then commonly used by scriveners producing hand-lettered manuscripts. This type so resembled hand lettering that the publishers felt it necessary to print a caution at the end of the Psalter. It stated: "This book was produced by a skillful invention for pressing and lettering without a pen or graver." Today we would label the Psalter of 1457 a fine art book or reproduction.

The first datable prints occur thirty or forty years before the Psalter of 1457. There is a Dutch Madonna from 1418 and a German St. Christopher dated 1423. These dated works suggest the very beginnings of the print industry and show that the intent and ability to make reproductions was part of the earliest history of printing.

Twenty years later, in 1477, in Southern Germany a print of St. Elizabeth of Hungary was pasted into a folio Augsburg Bible. Like many similiar images of that era, the print was made from two blocks. Part of the image recorded on one of the blocks included the saint's face, hands and her name in script. The second block contained details of her torso, dress and the background. What is revealing about this print is that when the two blocks were printed, a thin, white line was left between the two pieces.

This thin, white line offers a clue to a different intent and ability: while some were trying to create reproductions by means of the printing process, others were using the same printing techniques to create images unique to the print medium. No drawing, painting or illuminated manuscript of that era would have produced a figure with some details separated from other details by a white line of blank space. This white line is in fact a negative space that does not print. It shows on the printed paper because of a solution for design unique to printing. It is a concept that only an artist familiar with printing would invent and use. That it was not hidden or covered over suggests an intentional creation of an image unique to printing. This white line is a clue to one of the first original prints.

In 1976 Gene Baro wrote in his introduction to the catalogue for *Thirty Years of American Printmaking:* "Printmaking becomes artistically important when its mediums are used singly or in combination to project visual statements that cannot be made by other means." This comment could apply to the images of the early fifteenth century as well as those of the late twentieth century. It is the intent of the visual statement that suggests the difference between an original print and a reproduction. If the intent is to replicate or suggest an image best created as a drawing, a painting or even hand lettering, it does not matter whether the technique used is hand drawn or photomechanical. The intent and the result is a reproduction in the tradition of the Psalter of 1457.

If, however, the intent is to project a visual statement that can only be made by printing, no matter whether the technique is hand drawn or photomechanical, then, in the tradition of the 1477 St. Elizabeth of Hungary, the work is an original print. The intent to make a reproduction is an achievement of printing, but the intent to make an original print is an achievement of art.

Richard Sewell

An Original Print

It has become necessary to qualify the description of a print as "original" because of the development of processes that have enabled the production of exact replica images, particularly using offset lithography. These "copies" imply the existence of an original of which the image is a facsimile.

The virtue of the original print is that it employs means of production that allow the artist to directly control and manipulate the image at every stage. The print results from a constant involvement of the artist with certain tools and materials. It is an original that exists in multiple form.

A single print should, therefore, be described as a proof or an impression and not as a copy. This distinction has led to a great deal of confusion among art dealers and the public as to the definition and proper marketing of original prints.

Nick Novak

Reproductions

Reproductions are images that have been photomechanically reproduced. Reproductions are not "original". The original is the work from which colour separations or photomechanical halftone negatives are produced. These photographic materials are then used to make large editions on commercial, high-volume printing equipment. This product is not "limited" in any way. If the original exists, any number or sets of reproductions can be produced. Even if the original source for the image has disappeared, more copies can be printed from stored plates or separations. In some cases reproductions can even be re-shot from an existing reproduction. It is not necessary for an artist to be involved in the process at all. The notion of a "limited edition" reproduction comes from the early days of printing when there were limitations inherent in various media. Many of those limitations have been overcome by chemical or technological improvements. Therefore, to label a reproduction as "limited edition" is erroneous.

Paul Feldman

A Definition of Printmaking

Traditionally, prints have been viewed as multiple images produced from a plate. The plate is an intermediary between the printmaker's conception and the print—a rigid, flat surface that contains the picture or message. This image receives ink, and the inked image is transferred to the paper by pressure. The process can be repeated many times to produce nearly exact copies. For centuries this definition remained valid, but contemporary developments have stimulated a much more expansive view of the meaning of printmaking. Today a print is more likely to be defined as a two- or three-dimensional image or form made by a process or combination of processes that may be repeated to produce multiple copies of even unique pieces.

As the medium itself keeps evolving, the definition of "printmaking" also seems to be constantly changing. Perhaps it would be appropriate to have a print disclosure sheet, which would include an itemized list of all processes related to printmaking. The artist would check off whatever processes were used to complete the image. By referring to the print disclosure sheet, the prospective buyer or critic could evaluate all aspects and attributes of each image produced and formulate his or her own value judgement of whether or not it is a "print".

Otis Tamasauskas

Syncopation (see cover) is an edition of fifty original prints. It is an example of a combination of two printmaking processes, etching (intaglio) and silkscreen, handpulled by the artist, Jan Winton. The first part of the printmaking process for this work was the production of the etched image on three zinc plates. The artist used hand-tool techniques and acid to produce the desired image area on the surface of the plates.

The artist has also used a stencil to handroll two colours, mauve and pink, onto two plate surfaces. The plates are now ready to print.

Black ink has been wiped into the deep impressions that mark the surface of the plate, and the excess has been wiped away. Ink now remains only in these image areas.

The plates are placed on the bed of the press, the pressure is set, and pre-moistened 100% rag paper is laid down over the plates.

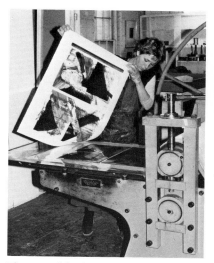
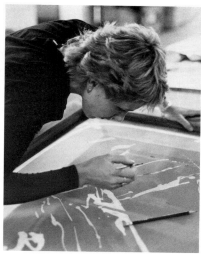

The press blankets are placed over the paper, and the print is "pulled" by turning the wheel of the press, allowing the bed to move through two rollers. The image is set and the paper is lifted. Fifty such etchings are pulled and allowed to dry before beginning the second process, silkscreening.

The three-colour (red, yellow and blue) screen image is printed over the etched image. Here the artist is blocking out areas on the screen that she does not want ink to pass through.

The enamel ink is worked to the correct consistency and then poured onto the screen ready for printing.

The ink is pulled across the screen by a squeegee and pushed through the open or image areas of the screen onto the paper below. Four "passes" were made for each colour on each print.

Syncopation has been used both as the image for the cover of the exhibition catalogue and as the image for the exhibition poster. Historically, posters have been considered advertisements or publicity containing type or commercial logos. They can be printed by hand in a limited-edition format or reproduced photo-mechanically.

Small posters advertising the sale of indulgences to finance the rescue of Constantinople from the Turks are among the earliest dated pieces of Gutenberg's typography. In the 1830s publishers in Paris began to advertise their illustrated books with large black and white lithographs drawn by the illustrators of the various books. Between 1866 and 1890 Jules Chéret became known for his hundreds of posters advertising theatres, music halls, cigarettes and champagne.

Early lithographic poster workshops in France exposed artists to the commercial printing media, and artists began to explore the possibilities of printmaking in their own work. By the last decade of the nineteenth century Bonnard, Vuillard and Toulouse-Lautrec had elevated the colour lithographic poster to the status of art.

An artist working in etching (intaglio) must first select the type of metal surface or plate that is appropriate for the image he or she wants to create. Many different metals are available, including copper, zinc and brass. Each has unique characteristics the printmaker can make use of. Copper is considered the premier metal for etching; it is a hard, pure element that will accept delicate, sensitive tones and lines. The durability and consistent grain of copper make it especially suited to processes such as dry point, mezzotint and engraving. Unfortunately, the scarcity and expense of copper make it a difficult material to acquire. Zinc plates are now commonly used as a less expensive and more readily available substitute for copper.

However, zinc is an alloy, a combination of soft and hard metals, which makes it difficult to engrave, dry point and mezzotint. The soft portions of the metal break down under printing pressures; delicate aquatints disappear; dry points break off and close up—all of which may yield unsatisfactorily small editions. But for the contemporary printmaker the alloy characteristics of this metal offer many interesting qualities of texture and line. Acid "bites" zinc rapidly, and the metal seems to be suited to etching processes in which the printmaker can achieve good line and tonal ranges.

After the type of plate is chosen, the plate edges must be bevelled to protect the printer's hands and the felt blankets of the press. The printmaker is then ready to select an approach to the desired image. Of the many approaches to intaglio printing there are three that are primarily line processes and closely connected to drawing techniques.

ENGRAVING

Engraving is the oldest of the intaglio processes. The printmaker uses a sharp tool called a burin to directly scratch, or engrave, into the surface of the metal plate. The plate is then inked and printed, with the ink that has been caught in the engraved lines forming the image. Variety of line is controlled by the width of the burin point and the depth to which the artist engraves the plate surface.

DRY POINT

In the dry point process the printmaker again works directly on the metal plate with a sharp needle, which leaves two "burrs" of metal on either side of the line. When the plate is wiped after inking, the ink remains caught in the burrs to form the image. Because of the great pressure exerted on the plate during printmaking, the burrs wear down rapidly and severely limit the number of acceptable prints that can be produced. This technical problem and the necessity of using expensive copper plates for dry point account for the limited popularity of this technique today.

ETCHING

Etching has become the most popular of intaglio processes for contemporary printmakers, and intaglio printing is often referred to simply as etching. The popularity of etching is largely due to two important factors: the variety of line and tone that can be achieved employing methods closely connected to both drawing and painting and the suitability of etching to a variety of metals. To begin this description of etching processes, we will start with the simple line etching technique.

In LINE ETCHING, a ground must first be put on the plate to coat the surface and protect it against corrosive acids. These grounds can be painted on with a soft brush or rolled on with a rubber roller. When the ground solidifies, the plate is ready to be drawn on, using a sharp, pointed needle or other instrument that will remove the ground cleanly. The artist draws the image with enough pressure to remove the ground, like a skater leaving a sharp, incised line on the ice.

The plate is then put into an acid bath; nitric acid, diluted to a suitable strength, is usually used. The acid only bites into the drawn areas, where the ground has been removed. The plate is left in the acid bath according to how dark and intense the artist wants the lines to be. The longer the plate is in the acid, the darker the lines will be.

Next the ground is washed off with a solvent. The plate is then "inked up", which means that the entire surface of the plate is covered with ink (any colour can be used). The ink is pushed into the etched lines with a soft dabber. The plate is then "wiped", using tarlatan or newsprint. The ink is removed flatly from the surface but is tenderly preserved in the etched lines.

When the surface is totally cleaned and polished, the press is set up. Soft felt blankets are positioned under the roller of the press, and the pressure is adjusted to 30.000 pounds per square inch. The inked plate is carefully placed on the bed of the press, and a sheet of damp paper with a high compressibility rating is registered over the plate. The felt blankets cover the paper and plate. Then the plate is "cranked" through the roller, which transfers pressure into the blankets, which in turn flex the soft, dampened paper into the etched lines beneath the surface of the plate. This pulls the ink out of the etched lines.

Once the plate has been through the roller of the press and the blankets are lifted, the paper is carefully peeled off the plate. The printed image is then viewed. Corrections can be made by scraping away lines with a knife. These areas are repaired by burnishing and polishing so that they blend in with the rest of the surface of the plate.

Because of the inherent smoothness of the etching plate surface, ink will not adhere to the plate in large sections and it is impossible to create wide areas of varying tones. To achieve values of tone, the printmaker must further manipulate the plate surface.

In the AQUATINT process the printmaker sprinkles a fine pulverized rosin dust evenly over selected areas of the clean plate. The rosin dust is usually sprinkled through cheesecloth, and the fineness of the dusting depends on the number of cheesecloth plies used. The spacing between each rosin particle will determine the fineness or coarseness of the aquatint. Next the plate is heated to 230° F, the temperature at which the rosin melts, turns into a liquid (hence "aqua") and adheres to the plate, forming a speckled "stop out" resistant to the acid. Now the plate is ready for the acid bath.

The longer the plate or areas of the plate are exposed to the acid, the deeper the bite will be around the particles of rosin. By controlling both the etching time factor and the amount of rosin dust applied, the printmaker can achieve an appreciable variety of tones. After the plate has been etched, the rosin is washed off with a solvent. The surface of the plate will now have a pitted texture like sandpaper, which will hold the ink. Tones can also be produced by burnishing and scraping the aquatint. These processes reduce the coarseness of the aquatinted surface so that it does not hold as much ink.

The MEZZOTINT process is similar to aquatint in that the plate is first manipulated to produce a solid textured surface that will print an even black. This is done by raising a metal burr evenly over the entire surface of the plate. The printmaker then scrapes and burnishes the plate, in varying degrees, back to the smoothness of the untreated plate to achieve areas of lesser tone. To produce a white line, the plate would be burnished to a polished surface that would no longer hold any ink.

To produce the greatest variety of line and tone in an intaglio print, most contemporary printmakers combine as many of these methods as necessary to achieve the desired image.

Otis Tamasauskas

The making of a screenprocess edition can be divided into eight steps: making the master, separating the colours, transferring the image to the screens, mixing the colours, paper preparation, proofing and printing the edition, curating and documentation.

Of these eight steps the first four are artistic and allow the artist infinite variety. The second four are technical and require skilled control by the printer. This process of making an edition allows for a distinction between artistic and technical problems, which gives an artist the opportunity to work with a printer who can be responsible for the technical aspects. However, this process can also enable the artist to assume both roles and, as a printmaker, function as both artist and printer.

The artistic steps are unlimited in their possibilities if the artist is familiar with the range of the screenprocess medium. To simplify this description of screenprocess, the technique referred to here is one of the most basic; it is called "tusche and glue". Screenprocess prints are seldom made with one colour, so we are "making" a two-colour print using the above method. The two colours are yellow and red.

1. MAKING THE MASTER
The master is a piece of paper the same size as the paper to be printed on in the edition. The image is drawn on this paper in the exact place that it will appear in the final print. Notations can be included for colour or texture and for materials or images helpful to the creation of the print.

2. SEPARATION OF THE COLOURS
Whatever the complexity of the master, the artist must simplify the image into two colours. This involves re-drawing and re-thinking the image into lines, shapes and textures compatible with the tusche and glue technique.

The artist creates the separation by placing two sheets of tracing paper over the master. One sheet will be for the yellow elements and one sheet for the red. If an area is to be orange, which is a combination of yellow and red, then the shape or line will appear on both sheets of tracing paper. The system for keeping these two sheets in line so that they eventually create the intended image is called registration.

Registration techniques can be very simple or very complicated depending on the degree of accuracy required. For this print we are using a very simple system of two X marks in the right and left margins of the master. We then trace these two marks onto both sheets of paper on top of the master. When the three sets of Xs are lined up, the sheets and master are in register.

3. TRANSFERRING THE COLOUR SEPARATIONS TO THE SCREENS
The image of the print will be achieved by printing the two elements of the design, one in yellow and one in red, from two screens. These designs are put onto the screens in the proper position by using the registration X marks on the two sheets of tracing paper. This is done by placing the yellow tracing under a screen and copying the design and the X marks onto the fabric. A second screen is placed on top of the red tracing, and the design and X marks are again copied onto the fabric. Because the X marks on the tracing paper were in register, the screens with the two separated elements of the design on them are now also in register.

The elements on both screens are painted with tusche, an oil-based painting medium, in those areas of the design through which ink is to print. These parts of the design are the positive areas. When the tusche has dried, the other areas of the design —those areas not to be printed—will be coated with the glue block-out material. These parts of the design are called the negative areas.

When both materials are dry, the screens are placed on a wash-out table and cleaned with a solvent that dissolves only the oil-based tusche. The glue part of the stencil is not affected during this cleaning and will be the stencil on the screen fabric that creates the image when printed. The screens now have a positive area that is open and a negative area that is closed. These positive and negative areas are in register on both screens and are now ready to be printed.

4. MIXING THE COLOURS
To judge the exact colour of screenprocess ink is possible only when the ink is printed and dry. To save time and to allow greater control over mixing colours, the inks are mixed in small quantities and proofed on a small proofing screen. These colour tests

are called swatches, and when dry, they allow colours to be examined more quickly than if the entire image had to be printed on the large screens and constantly cleaned from trial to trial. When the correct colour and transparency are found, the ink is mixed in the amount necessary to print the edition.

5. PAPER PREPARATION

Usually some time has to be spent getting the paper ready to print. There should be enough paper for the edition plus various proofs, such as artist's proofs, archival proofs and the proofs lost through mistakes in printing or handling. Sometimes special care has to be taken to achieve exact registration. This may include trimming one edge of the paper or placing pencil lines on the paper to allow for visual positioning on the printing table.

6. PROOFING AND PRINTING THE EDITION

Now that the design, screens, stencils, ink and paper have been prepared, the print can be proofed. The screen for the first colour, yellow, is clamped onto a printing table, and paper is registered under the screen using the X marks as guides. The yellow ink, which has already been mixed and proofed on the small screen, is now printed through the stencil onto the proofing paper and a few sheets of the paper to be used in the final edition. These proofs are allowed to dry, and the screen is cleaned, leaving the stencil intact. The screen and stencil can then be stored.

The second screen with the red stencil on it is now clamped onto a printing table, and one of the yellow proofs is registered under it. This is done by using the tracing for the yellow stencil with the X mark on it. When the image and stencil are in register, the red ink is printed on top of the yellow proofs. The proofs are allowed to dry, and the red screen is cleaned and stored with the stencil intact.

By checking these proofs, the artist can determine whether any changes need to be made in the registration, stencil, ink or paper. If everything is as intended, the edition is printed. The process is the same as proofing, but now all the paper is printed.

7. CURATING THE EDITION

Curating involves checking all the printed proofs and discarding those not of edition quality. The approved proofs are then assembled into the prints in the edition plus whatever additional proofs are to be kept. This latter category includes artist's proofs, printer's proofs and studio or archival proofs. All the prints are signed, numbered and recorded on the back with a catalogue number that corresponds to a number on the documentation sheet for the entire edition.

8. DOCUMENTATION

Documentation consists of a sheet containing a record of all the specifics of the production of the edition. This includes the names of the artist and printer, the dates of production, the ink and paper used, the number of proofs in the edition and any other information of technical or historical interest.

Richard Sewell

The hand lithographic process differs from other print processes in that no physical abrasion or alteration of the printing surface is required to create the separation of image and non-image areas. This is accomplished using the special properties of lithographic limestone or prepared zinc or aluminum plates. Drawing can be done directly on the printing surface using lithographic crayons and tusche or transferred from a specially prepared paper. Photographic images can also be applied to stone and plate. Alterations and additions can be done throughout the process.

If a stone is to be used, it must first be prepared by graining. Using a fine abrasive, the printmaker removes all old images from the stone so that a clear surface and a fine tooth remain. Preparatory drawing can be done on tracing paper, and a neutral non-printing outline can be transferred to the surface of the stone as a guide. Depending on his or her needs, the artist can choose to disregard this procedure and work directly on the stone surface.

All tools for drawing must be greasy or eventually be converted to a grease base in order to become fixed on the stone or plate. Grease will react chemically with lithographic limestone and cause it to attract grease until a layer of the stone is removed by graining. Lithographic limestone will also absorb water and can be made to attract water consistently if it is treated with acid carried in a gum arabic solution. After the drawing is completed, this solution is applied to the entire surface of the stone.

The printing process in lithography depends on the separation of image areas as grease receptive and non-image areas as water receptive. During printing, a thin film of water is applied to the surface of the stone with a sponge. The oil-based ink on the inking roller will be attracted to the grease (drawn) areas of the stone and repelled by the water adhering to the non-image areas. Paper must be registered in position on the stone and pressure applied from a press. The stone must be re-inked after every impression is pulled.

Nick Novak

1. Graining the stone, using a smaller stone

2. Drawing directly onto the stone, using a lithographic pencil

3. Sponging water onto the surface of the stone

4. Rolling ink onto the surface of the stone

5. Paper is positioned over the surface of the stone, and registration marks are drawn in.

6. Paper, over which a tympan is placed, and the inked stone are cranked through the press.

7. Pulling the printed sheet of paper away from the stone

8. Viewing the printed sheet

The following are personal statements written by three artists at Open Studio. Intended to give impressionistic views of printmaking, the statements, like the artists, are varied and distinctive.

The Print

In *Webster's New World Dictionary* between the words *prink* and *printed circuit* lies the word *print*:

print (print), **n.** [<OFr.< *prient*, pp. of *preindre*< L. *premere*, to press], 1. a mark made on a surface by pressing or hitting with an object; imprint: as, the *print* of a heel. 2. an object for making such a mark, as stamp, die, etc. 3. a cloth printed with a design, or a dress made of this. 4. the condition of being printed. 5. printed letters, words, etc.; the impression made by inked type. 6. a picture or design printed from a plate, block, etc., as an etching or lithograph. 7. a photograph made by exposing sensitized paper to light passed through a negative. **v.t.** 1. to make a print on or in. 2. to stamp (a mark, letter, etc.) on or in a surface. 3. to produce on (paper, etc.) the impression of inked type, plates, etc. by means of a printing press. 4. to produce (a book, etc.) by typesetting, presswork, binding, etc. 5. to publish (a manuscript, etc.) in print. 6. to write in letters resembling printed ones. 7. to produce (a photograph), by exposing sensitized paper to light passed through a negative. 8. to impress upon the mind, memory, etc. **v.i.** 1. to practice the trade of a printer. 2. to produce an impression, photograph, etc. 3. to draw letters resembling printed ones.—**in** (or **out of**) **print**, still (or no longer) procurable for purchase from the publisher: said of books, etc.—**print'a·ble, adj.**—**print'er, n.***

*With permission. From *Webster's New World Dictionary*, Concise Edition. Copyright 1964 by The World Publishing Company.

All of these definitions of the word *print* are exactly how I would define what a print is. The only definition I would add to all of those above is that a print can be a work of art. Once an artist becomes involved in the printing process, painting process or any other process, there is a very good chance that a work of art will be produced. It doesn't always happen, but sometimes it does. When an artist produces a work with the printing process, the resulting work is what I would call a print. I would like to see that definition added to the dictionary.

Don Holman

Intaglio

Imagine that you are a hard metal plate sleeping comfortably in your own molecular structure. Along comes a layer of waxy varnish and spreads itself on top of you. Next a hard needle scrapes through your blanket of varnish, tickling your ribs and exposing lines of metal. It's not Saturday, but they give you a bath anyway —and this bath is acid. The acid eats into your exposed areas, creating enormous caverns, riverbeds, plateaux and broad plains. A geography of image is formed. After successive protective coats and plunges into acid, you are cleaned up so that nothing remains but your shiny metal—now in the form of an image. Someone has given you a personality beyond your metalness. That might be satisfaction enough: call it sculpture if you like. You feel complete but…

Imagine that great gobs of black ink suddenly blot out the sky. The oily tidal wave unfolds over your whole surface and is pushed down and settles into every pore. Luckily, someone comes along immediately and begins to clean you with cloths and hands, wiping up the excess ink. The smoother textured areas allow some ink to remain, while the deep gorges are full. The wiping creates a variety of shadows over your geography—long shadows by the edges of your mountains, deep bottomless shadows in your canyons, while the very tops of your landscape are bright and clean and shiny.

Imagine also that you are a vast sheet of white paper, a web of cellulose tubes clinging and intermeshed one upon the other. Water softens and relaxes you. You're feeling clean and ready to go, but you don't know who you are—only what you're made of.

You're placed gently over the metal plate (remember, that's you too!), and soft blankets of wool are smoothed over you. Nice time for napping, huh? Nope. The wheels turn and off you go under the crush of enormous pressure in the press. Your fibres are flattened and seem to flow into any available crevice, and the ink is pushed into you and blended with your being. Slowly the crush lessens and the blankets are lifted up. Hands pick up your corners and carry you away to dry. The paper part of you keeps the memory of the experience and the metal part of you is inked all over again, ready for the next print, ready to create another mirror image in both texture and composition.

Prints are ghosts of the performing act of image making, full of illusions of depth and space and populated with personal mythologies—clues to the mystery of art and experience. When I look at a Rembrandt self-portrait, with a quizzical grin etched onto his mischievous face, I know we share a secret.

Brian Kelley

Screenprocess

Screenprocess printing, also called silkscreen or serigraphy, is a stencil printing technique. The stencil is comprised of a fabric stretched on a wooden frame and a block-out medium placed on the fabric. This placement creates the design to be printed. In printing, the ink is forced across the fabric and through the areas not blocked out. This ink prints an impression on the paper under the stencil.

Stencil printing is older than lithography, intaglio and even relief or woodblock printing methods. Although not firmly documented, the beginning of stencil techniques can be traced to China around A.D. 500. Stencil process printing in various forms has occurred throughout the last 1500 years in the East as well as the West.

In the 1400s relatively simple techniques were used by printers in Italy to stencil colour onto completed images pulled from relief blocks. By the late 1800s in France fabrics were being printed with screens stretched with silk similar to the technique used today. By the 1800s stencil printers in Japan had developed a very complex matrix similar to the fabric support currently used in screenprocess. Their method was to glue elements of the design together with hair or silk threads. This allowed for complex designs with floating shapes within shapes, a vast improvement over the Chinese stencil, which allowed only a silhouette solution to their images.

In the twentieth century the history of screenprocess printing is more specific, with individual artists and printers giving their names to various techniques. In England in 1907 the first patent for screenprocess was granted to Samuel Simson, a printer in Manchester. In the United States one of the first artists to gain recognition as a silkscreen practitioner was Anthony Velonis. During the 1930s a Works Projects Administration silkscreen printing venture under his direction first introduced many artists to the screenprocess technique as a fine art.

In the past twenty years screenprocess printing—as well as lithography and intaglio—has contributed to the growth of interest in printmaking. The ability of this technique to print a broad range of colours from the subtlest transparency to the densest opaqueness and its ability to print on a wide range of surfaces from paper to plastic and glass have made screenprocess printing — the oldest of the printing processes —the newest discovery of artists and collectors in the print renaissance of the last quarter-century.

Richard Sewell

BIOGRAPHIES OF THE ARTISTS

Sandra Altwerger
Born: Toronto, 1942
Sandra Altwerger studied at the Ontario College of Art, where she now teaches. She also studied in Provincetown, Mass., and Mexico. Since 1963 Altwerger has participated in numerous group shows, received purchase awards and grants and has had solo exhibitions. Her work is in many collections across Ontario, and she is represented by Open Studio and Gallery Moos, Toronto.

Kim Andrews
Born: Saskatchewan, 1939
Kim Andrews was educated at the University of Alberta and the City University of New York. He has been represented in various group exhibitions. His work is in the Owens Art Gallery and Art Bank.

Jacques Benoît
Born: Montreal, 1946
Jacques Benoît studied at various institutions in Montreal, including l'Atelier du Frère Jérôme and l'Ecole des Beaux-Arts. Since 1965 he has been in many exhibitions in Ontario and Quebec.

Mel Benson
Born: Rama Ojibwa Indian Reserve, Rama, Ontario, 1951
Mel Benson studied under Indian artist Arthur Shilling and at Central Technical School, Toronto. He has been featured in group exhibitions, and his work is in university and government art collections.

Don Carr
Born: Toronto, 1944
Don Carr studied at the Ontario College of Art, the University of Guelph and the University of Chicago. His work is included in public art gallery collections. Since 1966 he has been represented in numerous Canadian and American print exhibitions.

Moira Clark
Born: Toronto, 1950
Moira Clark was educated at York University and has been exhibiting extensively since 1972. She is represented in collections in Canada and England. She has numerous dealers, including Open Studio and the Aggregation Gallery, Toronto.

Susan Farquhar
Born: North Bay, Ont., 1954
Susan Farquhar studied at the University of Guelph and York University. She has been in group shows and presently is the assistant director of lithography at Open Studio.

Paul Feldman
Born: Leeds, England, 1948
Paul Feldman attended St. Lawrence College in Kingston, Ont. His work is in many corporate, public gallery and private collections. Since 1975 he has exhibited in numerous group shows in Canada and the United States. Presently he is assistant director of screenprocess at Open Studio.

Zenji Funabashi
Born: Tokyo, Japan, 1942
Zenji Funabashi studied at the Tama Fine Art University in Tokyo. He has been employed as a commercial artist and has been exhibiting since 1975.

Robert Game
Born: Edmonton, Alberta, 1944
Robert Game received his BFA from the University of Alberta. He has exhibited in many solo and group shows in Canada and the United States. In 1977 he received a commission from Xerox of Canada for an edition of etchings. His work is in various corporate and government art collections, and he has several published editions of prints.

Yves Gaucher
Born: Montreal, 1934
Yves Gaucher is a self-educated painter and print-maker. Since 1957 he has travelled extensively in Mexico, Europe, Canada, Egypt, North Africa and South America. His work has been exhibited internationally, including Canada, Europe and Japan. Gaucher is married with two sons and is an associate professor at Concordia University.

Judy Gouin
Born: England, 1947
Judy Gouin attended the Chelsea School of Art, London, England. Since 1972 she has exhibited extensively, including the Graphex I, II, III, 5, 6 and 7 Exhibitions, the 4th and 6th British International Print Biennale and numerous other group shows, as well as many solo exhibitions. Her work is in many public art gallery, corporate and private collections across Canada. Gouin has also received various grants and purchase awards. She is represented by Open Studio; Mira Godard Gallery, Toronto; and Gallery Graphics, Ottawa.

Elizabeth Hague
Born: Montreal, 1950
Elizabeth Hague received her BFA from Sir George Williams University, Montreal, in 1971. Since then she has been exhibiting in solo and group shows. Her work is represented in Art Bank, the Toronto-Dominion Bank and other collections.

Barbara Hall
Born: New York, 1942
Barbara Hall received her BFA from the Art Institute of Chicago in 1967, and has studied in Florence, Italy. She has been in many print exhibitions, including the XI and XII Premi Internacional Dibiux Joan Miro in Barcelona and Madrid. She has received grants, purchase awards and is in gallery and bank collections. Hall is a co-founder of Open Studio. She is represented by the Mira Godard Gallery, Toronto; Gallery Graphics, Ottawa; and Portland Gallery, Manchester, England.

Carol Heimpel

Born: Kitchener, Ont., 1945
Carol Heimpel studied at Central Technical School, Toronto, and has worked as a commercial artist. She has exhibited through Open Studio group exhibitions and is in the Gallery O collection, Toronto.

Don Holman

Born: Kansas City, Missouri, 1946
Don Holman received his BFA in 1968 from the Kansas City Art Institute. Since 1976 he has exhibited in Canada, the United States and Mexico. His work is in various public gallery, corporate, bank and government collections. Holman is represented by Open Studio and Gallery Moos, Toronto. He is co-director of lithography at Open Studio.

Nikolette Jakovac

Born: St. Louis, Missouri, 1940
Nikolette Jakovac received her BFA in 1965 from the Washington University School of Fine Arts. She has been exhibiting with Open Studio since 1971 and has participated in other group shows.

Denise Job

Born: Toronto, 1952
Denise Job graduated from the Ontario College of Art in 1975. Since then she has participated in various group exhibitions across Ontario and was also in the 7th International Miniature Print Exhibition in New York in 1979.

Brian Kelley

Born: 1956
Brian Kelley studied at the Pratt Institute in Brooklyn, New York, and received his BFA in graphic arts in 1968. Since then he has freelanced as a designer, taught printmaking and bookbinding and travelled in Europe, North Africa and Asia. Kelley is now director of etching at Open Studio. He has exhibited in the United States, Europe and Canada. His work is in various collections, and there are many published editions of Kelley's prints.

Harold Klunder

Born: Holland, 1943
Since 1976 Harold Klunder has been in many group shows, primarily in Ontario. He has had numerous solo exhibitions, beginning with Hart House, University of Toronto, in 1974 and, most recently, the Sable-Castelli Gallery, Toronto. He has often participated in the Art Gallery of Ontario "Artists with their Work" program. Klunder is featured in gallery and bank collections and is represented by the Sable-Castelli Gallery, Toronto.

William Kurelek

Born: Alberta, 1927   Died: Toronto, 1977
William Kurelek studied at the University of Manitoba and briefly at art schools in Toronto and Mexico. He had many solo exhibitions in Canada, including thirteen shows at Toronto's Isaacs Gallery. Kurelek participated in group exhibitions in Canada and the United States and won many awards. He illustrated numerous books, some of which he also wrote, and executed many murals. His work is in many public gallery collections. The estate of William Kurelek is represented by the Isaacs Gallery.

John Lander

Born: Canada, 1951
John Lander graduated from York University in 1974. He has received grants and is represented in a number of gallery collections. Lander has been showing in selected group exhibitions since 1973, including, most recently, shows at the Nancy Poole Gallery in Toronto and the London Regional Art Gallery.

Terry Legault

Born: Toronto, 1956
Terry Legault studied at the University of Guelph and has been published by Sword Street Press and Three Schools. She has shown in group exhibitions and has work in private and gallery collections, including the Art Gallery of Hamilton.

Rita Letendre

Born: Drummondville, P.Q., 1928
Rita Letendre studied painting and printmaking at l'Ecole des Beaux Art, Montreal, and studied with Paul-Emile Borduas. She has had many solo exhibitions, including a show at Gallery Moos in Toronto and a travelling show organized by the Museum of Fine Arts, Montreal. She has also been in many group shows and has received various commissions. She is represented in all major museums in Canada, museums in the United States, many universities and many business, industry and government collections.

Lorna Livey

Born: Quebec City, P.Q., 1951
Lorna Livey received her BFA from York University in 1973. She has exhibited in numerous group shows throughout Canada, including the Mira Godard Gallery in Toronto, and had a solo exhibition in 1975 at the University of Toronto. Her work is in corporate and private collections. Livey is represented by Open Studio and Mira Godard in Toronto; the Solander Case, Niagara-on-the-Lake; and the Fleet Gallery, Winnipeg.

Eugene Mazzei

Born: Detroit, Michigan, 1945
Eugene Mazzei received his BFA from Sir George Williams University, Montreal, and also studied in Detroit and San Francisco. He has been in many Canadian group exhibitions, including Pollock Gallery and Open Studio shows, and he has received a number of awards.

Louis de Niverville

Born: 1933
Louis de Niverville has exhibited extensively since 1957. His most recent solo exhibition was a major retrospective, organized by the Robert McLaughlin Gallery, which travelled to fourteen Canadian exhibition centres in 1978-1979, including the Art Gallery of Ontario. His work is in many gallery collections. De Niverville has also received numerous commissions for murals, including one at the Toronto International Airport and an Expo 67 theatre mural.

Nicholas Novak
Born: Yugoslavia, 1954
Nicholas Novak studied at York University and at the Ontario College of Art. He has won several awards and grants. His most recent exhibitions have been a group show at the Robert McLaughlin Gallery, Oshawa, and a solo show at Gallery 76, Toronto. He is co-director of lithography at Open Studio.

Mark Prent
Born: Montreal, 1947
Mark Prent received his BFA from Sir George Williams University, Montreal, in 1970. Since then he has had many solo and group exhibitions, most recently at the SAW Gallery, Ottawa, and in Holland and Germany. He has received many awards, and his work is in government and gallery collections. Prent is represented by the Isaacs Gallery, Toronto.

Erica Rutherford
Erica Rutherford has been in over one hundred group shows in Europe and North America since 1957. She has had numerous solo shows and has work in many gallery and corporate collections.

Hans Schweizer
Born: St. Peterzell, Switzerland, 1942
Hans Schweizer studied with J. Friedlander and L. Coutant in Paris. Since 1967 he has been in many international graphic exhibitions, has had numerous solo shows and has won many awards. Schweizer is represented by Gallery Moos, Toronto.

Richard Sewell
Born: St. Louis, Missouri, 1942
Richard Sewell was educated in Missouri and Mexico. He is a co-founder of Open Studio and the director of the screenprocess department. He has participated in many group shows, most recently in the invitational Bradford Biennale in England. Sewell's work is in bank and gallery collections and various private collections in Canada, the United States, Mexico and Europe.

James B. Spencer
Born: Wolfville, Nova Scotia, 1940
James Spencer studied at Acadia University in Wolfville and later graduated from the Ontario College of Art. He has exhibited through Open Studio group shows and at Hart House, the University of Toronto, and has work in the National Gallery of Canada.

Otis Tamasauskas
Born: Terschenreuth, Germany, 1947
Otis Tamasauskas studied at Central Technical School, Toronto; received his BFA from the University of Windsor in 1974; and has been on the staff at Open Studio. He has been in numerous group shows, including Graphex, and is represented by Open Studio and Mira Godard in Toronto. His work is in many bank, gallery and corporate collections.

Joy Walker
Born: Tacoma, Washington, 1942
Joy Walker studied at the University of Oregon, the University of Paris, Columbia University and the New York Studio School. She has had many solo shows since 1970 and has often participated in group shows. Her work is included in the collection of Art Bank and the Art Gallery of Ontario.

Jan Winton
Born: Toronto, 1954
Jan Winton received her BFA from the University of Waterloo in 1976 and also studied in Australia. She has been exhibiting since 1977 in group shows. Winton won the Open Studio Commemorative Print Edition Competition for her print, *Syncopation*.

All works in the touring exhibition are indicated by an asterisk.
Works are measured according to paper size. Height precedes width, and all measurements are given in inches.
All prints have been printed by the artist, except where the name of the printer(s) is given as the fifth line of an entry.
The symbol OS followed by a number indicates the Open Studio archive number.

*Mel Benson
Our Elder, 1976
19-1/4 x 14-1/2
etching
B. Kelley, P. Todd
OS 682

*Moira Clark
Full Moonlight, 1979
22 x 19
etching
OS 1279

*Moira Clark
Day Glow, 1980
30 x 22-1/4
etching
OS 1338

*Nikolette Jakovac
Garden, 1973
22 x 30
etching
OS 276

*Nikolette Jakovac
Dry Tangerines, 1974
20 x 22
etching
OS 352

*Denise Job
Phases of the Heart, 1978
6 x 8
etching
OS 1073

*Brian Kelley
The James River, Va., 1977
12-1/2 x 16-1/2
etching
OS 773

*Brian Kelley
Peeled Apple, 1976
8 x 9
etching
OS 591

*Terry Legault
Triumph (Triptych), 1979
30 x 66
etching
OS 1088

*Lorna Livey
Piano Window, 1978
30 x 22
etching
OS 1024

*Lorna Livey
Elmira Parlour Couch, 1979
15 x 17-1/2
etching
OS 1100

*Eugene Mazzei
Untitled, 1974
23 x 26
etching
OS 175

*Hans Schweizer
(Charlotte), 1973
39-1/2 x 28
etching
OS 227

*Otis Tamasauskas
Horn, 1977
27 x 28
etching and lithograph
OS 914

*Jan Winton
Syncopation, 1980
Open Studio Commemorative Edition
22 x 30
etching and screenprocess
OS 1397

*Sandra Altwerger
Wild Iris, 1977
22 x 30-1/4
screenprocess
OS 798

*Sandra Altwerger
Barbados Canefield, 1979
41 x 29-1/2
screenprocess
OS 1106

*Sandra Altwerger
Beaver Slide, 1979
35 x 45
screenprocess
OS 1222

*Kim Andrews
Untitled, 1973 (suite of four prints)
20 x 20, each print of suite
screenprocess
artist, R. Sewell
OS 101, 102, 103, 104
(This suite does not photograph well enough for reproduction.)

*Judy Gouin
Trees in Meadow, 1979
30 x 30
screenprocess
OS 1079

*Judy Gouin
Stumps, 1979
29-1/2 x 38-1/2
screenprocess
OS 1201

*Judy Gouin
December Ice, 1980
26-1/2 x 35-1/2
screenprocess
OS 1264

*Barbara Hall
Oasis, 1979
22 x 30
screenprocess
OS 1203

*Carol Heimpel
Shojo I, 1977
14-1/2 x 11-1/2
screenprocess and lithograph
OS 803

*John Lander
Coloured Dog Fish, 1978
41 x 29-1/2
screenprocess
OS 977

*Rita Letendre
Orani, 1978
40 x 30
screenprocess
R. Sewell, P. Feldman
OS 975

*Mark Prent
Untitled, 1974
41 x 29
screenprocess
R. Sewell, P. Feldman, J. Gouin
OS 384

*Erica Rutherford
Still Life with Red, 1978
30 x 22-1/4
screenprocess
artist, P. Feldman
OS 979

*Richard Sewell
Stopwatch, 1979
22-1/2 x 35
screenprocess
artist, N. Novak, V. Sharp
OS 1124

*Richard Sewell
Starbuck/Sewell Suite I Blue, 1976
44 x 30
screenprocess
artist, B. Kelley, F. Starbuck
OS 588

*Richard Sewell
Starbuck/Sewell Suite II Pink, 1975
44 x 30
screenprocess
artist, F. Starbuck
OS 490

*Joy Walker
Untitled, 1973
22 x 30
screenprocess
OS 293

*Jacques Benoît
Diagonal, 1980
26 x 19-1/2
lithograph
OS 1353

*Don Carr
U.F.O., 1974
41 x 29-1/2
lithograph
D. Holman, R. Sewell, E. Zingraff
OS 346

*Yves Gaucher
Jericho/An Allusion to Barnett Newman, 1978
29-1/4 x 41-1/2
lithograph
D. Holman, O. Tamasauskas, N. Novak
OS 1052

*Elizabeth Hague
Undine, 1980
22 x 30
lithograph
OS 1294

*Elizabeth Hague
The Park Entrance 2nd Version, 1980
30 x 40
lithograph
OS 1346

*Don Holman
Southern Ontario, 1980
42 x 28
lithograph
OS 1270

*Harold Klunder
Elderslie, 1980
30 x 40
lithograph
N. Novak, S. Farquhar
OS 1144

*Harold Klunder
Ivory Coast, 1979
33 x 24
lithograph
N. Novak
OS 1082

*William Kurelek
Children Schoolbound in Northern B.C., 1974
28 x 22
lithograph
D. Holman, E. Zingraff
OS 376

*Louis de Niverville
Moonlighting, 1979
22-1/2 x 28
lithograph
N. Novak, S. Farquhar, P. Feldman
OS 1196

*James B. Spencer
Reverse Wave, 1973
18 x 23
lithograph
D. Holman, E. Zingraff, S. McKenzie
OS 139

*Otis Tamasauskas
Japan Fan No. 6, 1980
30 x 40
lithograph and etching
OS 1351

Paul Feldman
The True North, 1975
26 x 20
screenprocess and etching
OS 453

Zenji Funabashi
Birds, 1977
22 x 30
screenprocess
OS 766

Robert Game
Gateway, 1979
30 x 22
etching
OS 1182

Robert Game
Within the Hill, 1979
22 x 30
etching
OS 1198

Susan Farquhar
Untitled Landscape, 1979
22 x 30
lithograph
OS 1056

Susan Farquhar
North West of Whitby, 1980
20 x 30
lithograph
OS 1259